PHOTOGRAPHY!

Text and photographs: Yvon Monette
Cover photograph: Nathalie Dumouchel, Studio Tormont
English translation: Catherine Solyom
Graphic Design: Zapp

This edition produced by DS-Max Inc.
250 Granton Drive
Richmond Hill, Ont. Canada

Printed in China

CONTENTS

OOOH,
THAT'S A
TIGHT SQUEEZE!

HELLO! LET ME INTRODUCE MYSELF.
MY NAME IS CLICK. PERHAPS YOU'VE HEARD OF ME?
WELL, YOU KNOW WHEN YOU WERE LITTLE, AND YOUR PARENTS WANTED
TO TAKE A PICTURE OF YOU, AND THEY SAID, "WATCH THE BIRDIE!"?
WELL, I'M THAT LITTLE BIRDIE. OF COURSE, NO ONE HAS EVER SEEN ME
BEFORE... I'M WHAT YOU'D CALL "CAMERA SHY." BUT NOW THAT IT'S
JUST YOU AND ME, AND I'M NICELY HIDDEN BETWEEN THE PAGES OF
THIS BOOK, I THINK IT'S SAFE TO COME OUT.

I SEE YOU HAVE A BRAND NEW CAMERA.
I THOUGHT I MIGHT HELP YOU GET TO KNOW IT AND DISCOVER
ITS MAGIC. YOU PROBABLY ALREADY KNOW THAT TO TAKE GOOD PICTURES
YOU NEED TO DO A LITTLE MORE THAN JUST POINT THE CAMERA AT SOMETHING
AND PRESS THE BUTTON. THERE ARE A FEW SIMPLE RULES THAT YOU HAVE TO
UNDERSTAND, AND THEY ARE ALL IN THIS BOOK — WITH PICTURES TO GUIDE
YOU THROUGH THE RIGHTS AND WRONGS OF PHOTOGRAPHY. SO OPEN YOUR
EYES, NICE AND WIDE, AND LOOK AT THE WORLD AROUND YOU. TAKE YOUR
CAMERA WITH YOU WHEREVER YOU GO, BE ON THE LOOKOUT, AND CLICK
AWAY! YOU WILL LEARN FROM YOUR MISTAKES AND YOU'LL BE
TAKING FANTASTIC PHOTOS IN NO TIME!

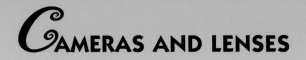

There are all kinds of cameras on the market today. Some of them are rather complicated to use and expensive, like single lens reflex cameras. With these cameras, you can take all kinds of pictures with separate lenses.

A **wide-angle lens** can fit more into the picture, giving you the impression of being farther away from your subject: it's the perfect lens for landscape photographs.

The view through a **standard lens** is much like the view from a human eye.

On the other hand, if you want to get closer to your subject without actually moving, you can use a **telephoto lens**. This lens is great for taking close-up photos.

But there are cameras that are much simpler to use, like the one that came with this book. You'll be able to have a lot of fun with this camera. It's a matter of getting to know it, and respecting its limits. It's called a *fixed focus 35 mm camera*: 'fixed focus' because you don't need to adjust the lens (depending on how far you are from the subject) to get sharp images on your photos;"35 mm" because the film you use in it is 35 mm wide.

YOUR CAMERA

This is a photo of your camera. You should learn the names of all of its parts and what they do before you start taking pictures. That way you won't waste your film...or your money!

Frame counter:
The number in this tiny little window tells you how many pictures you have already taken.

Rewind lever:
Winds your film clockwise back into the cassette after all the pictures have been taken.

Viewfinder:
This is the front of the viewfinder. Look through the opposite end to see what will be in the photograph.

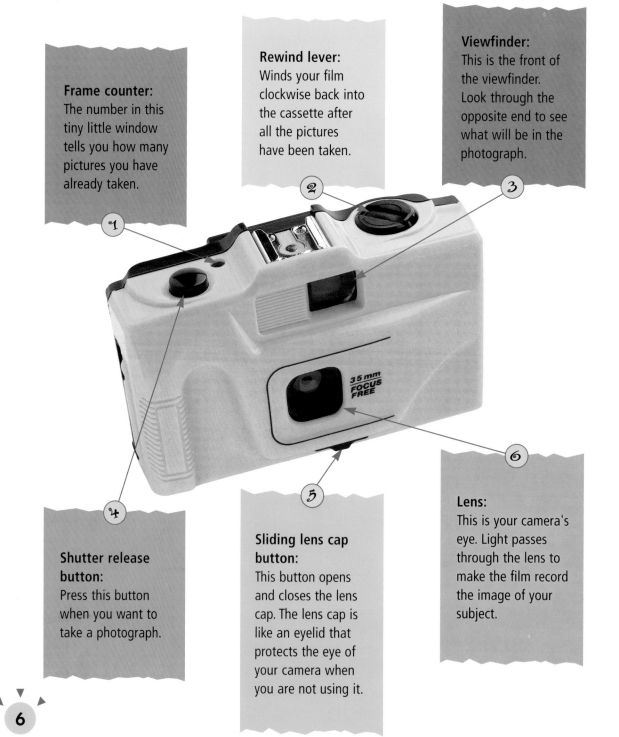

Shutter release button:
Press this button when you want to take a photograph.

Sliding lens cap button:
This button opens and closes the lens cap. The lens cap is like an eyelid that protects the eye of your camera when you are not using it.

Lens:
This is your camera's eye. Light passes through the lens to make the film record the image of your subject.

Film cassette holder:
This is where you place a new roll of film inside your camera.

7

Film wind-on:
Every time you take a picture, you have to turn this knob as far as it will go so that you can take another picture.

8

Take-up spool:
Every time you take a picture, the used film will wind onto this spool.

9

11

10

Door release button:
This opens the back of your camera so that you can take a roll of film out and put another one in. But you should NEVER open this door before you have taken all the pictures and rewound your film. The light could ruin your photos or the film that's left.

Rewind button:
When you have taken all your photos, press this button, and then turn the rewind lever (2) to wind the film back into its cassette.

HOLDING YOUR CAMERA

Look at these two pictures of the same subject: one is sharp and the other is blurred — the film has recorded the movement of the camera. To avoid this problem, hold the camera firmly with both hands and keep your arms tucked in close to your body.

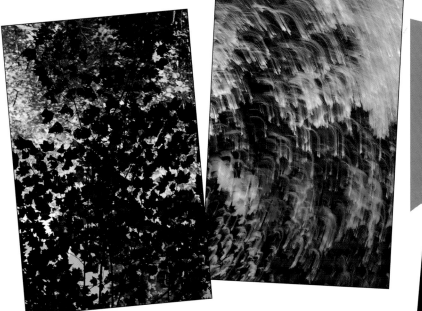

To keep the camera steady, you can prop your elbows on a table or press the camera against your nose! Then press the shutter release button gently, so that you don't move the camera.

You should not hold the camera like this. This boy has got his finger in front of the lens, and with his wings out like that, he really looks like a strange bird!

Now that's good picture-taking posture!

DON'T WORRY, YOU'LL GET THE HANG OF IT!

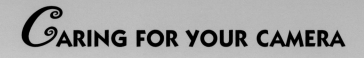

Your camera is not a toy. If you follow a few simple rules and handle it carefully, it will last you a long time.

Take especially good care of the lens. Remember, it is your camera's eye. If you keep it clean, your photos will be clean, too. Remove any dust with a blower brush, or with any kind of brush that has fine, soft bristles, and rub the surface of the lens very gently with a soft cloth. NEVER put your fingers on the lens.

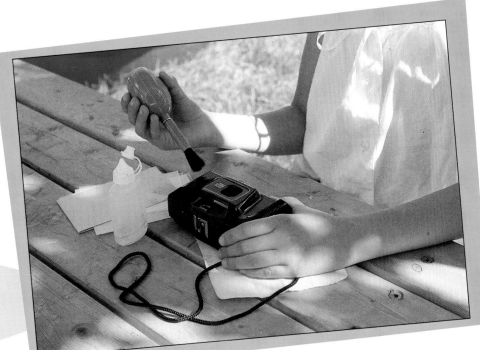

Take good care of your camera.

Be sure to close the lens cap before you put your camera away. Your camera is fragile so avoid rough handling.

You can make a case for it with a little padded box, or you can purchase an inexpensive one at a camera store. Don't forget — you can also store your camera in the box of your Camera Kit.

Avoid exposing your camera to excessive temperatures. For example, never leave your camera in direct sunlight on the seat of the car; the heat could ruin your film.

If you are not going to take any pictures for a long time, store your camera in a dry place and cover it so that it will not collect any dust. Be very careful when you are at the beach. Sand is a camera's worst enemy!

ILM

What is film? Well, it is a long strip of jelly-like plastic, with special chemicals on one side that react to light. When you press the shutter release button, the shutter, which is like a curtain, opens briefly to let in just enough light to expose the bit of film behind the lens. Because the light that enters your camera is reflected off your subject, the image of your subject is recorded on the film.

When all the pictures have been taken, the film is exposed to different chemicals in the laboratory that develop the images into photographs.

Just as there are many different cameras on the market, there are many different kinds of film. Your camera uses 35 mm film. You can choose color or black and white film, for prints or slides. Slide film is not very practical unless you have a slide projector. Black and white film can be very interesting, but to get the best results, you need to be able to develop the film yourself and make your own enlargements. Perhaps later you can set up your own mini photo lab at home?

In the meantime, it is best to stick with color film that is first developed into negatives, then printed on paper. It is the most common and practical film to use, and it is also the least expensive.

You can choose the number of frames on a roll (12, 24 or 36), and the film's sensitivity to light (100 ISO, 200 ISO, 400 ISO, etc.).

 FILM SPEED

The ISO number on the box of film tells you its degree of sensitivity to light. The bigger the number, the more the film reacts to light. Number 400 film, for example, is fast; it is used when there is less light available – inside, or on a cloudy day.

The smaller the ISO number, the less sensitive the film is. Number 100 film, for example, is slow, which means you need more light to make it react. This film is used on bright sunny days, or with a flash.

Use 400 ISO film for an indoor shot.

Use 100 ISO film for a bright sunny day.

FOR NOW, IT'S A GOOD IDEA TO USE THE MORE COMMON FILM SPEEDS: 100 OR 400 ISO. TAKE A GOOD LOOK AT HOW MUCH LIGHT IS AVAILABLE BEFORE YOU MAKE YOUR CHOICE.

LOADING YOUR FILM

The first thing you need to do is place your film properly in the camera. This is called loading your film. Follow each step in order, and use the illustration as a guide.

Before your first "click":

1. Slide the door release button down (**a**). The door will open and you will see an "S" for Start in the frame counter.

2. Insert the roll of 35 mm film in its place (**b**); pull about 3 inches (8 cm) of film out of the cassette and insert the end bit into one of the slits of the take-up spool (**d**).

3. Make sure that the notches along the bottom of the film fit into the slit at the bottom of the camera. Then, with your thumb, turn the film wind-on (**c**) as far as you can. With the door still open, press down on the shutter release button. Turn the wind-on again and release the shutter once more.

4. Carefully close the back door of the camera. Then advance the film until the frame counter reads "1." Now you are ready to take your first picture.

> HERE IS A TRICK TO MAKE SURE THAT YOUR FILM IS ADVANCING PROPERLY: IF THE REWIND LEVER TURNS BY ITSELF EVERY TIME YOU WIND THE FILM (c), YOUR FILM IS BEING WOUND CORRECTLY ONTO THE TAKE-UP SPOOL (d).

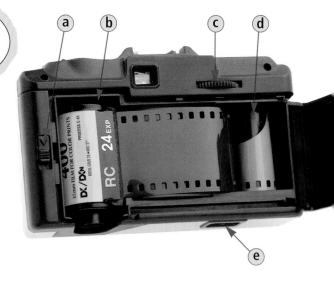

After your last "click":

5. After all the pictures have been taken, you will not be able to release the shutter any more, and the film wind-on (**c**) will not turn. Press down on the rewind button (**e**) and turn the rewind lever to wind the film back into its cassette. When the lever is loose and turns very easily, all the film has been rewound.

6. Now you can open the back door by sliding the button down (**a**). Take the film out. Never put in or take out a film in direct sunlight. The strong light can get into the cassette and ruin your photos.

7. Now for the best part! It's time to get your film developed. You can choose how your photos will be printed, on matte or glossy paper. Ask to see some examples before you make your choice. You can also choose the format.

Do you know what 'photography' really means? It comes from two Greek words: *phos*, meaning light, and *graphos*, which means drawing. So photography is like drawing with light. A photographer needs light just as a painter needs paint.

Take a look at how light 'lights up' the people and the things around you. Can you see how it is different in every case? Whether it is natural light, artificial light, or a combination of the two, it can be soft or hard, warm or cold. Light is what gives a photo its particular character and atmosphere.

From the front...

Notice how the position of the light creates different shadows. The sun lights up this little girl in three different ways:

...from the side

... and from the back.

Look at where the shadows fall.

The time of day and the weather also affect the quality of the light.

The morning sun gives off a bluish light.

At noon, the sun throws dark shadows over parts of this boy's face.

This room is flooded with the warm light of the late afternoon sun.

The setting sun brings out the texture of the fields.

The sun near the horizon splashes a beautiful yellow light onto this building.

The sun piercing through a stormy sky always has a dramatic effect.

This view of a port calls to mind the calm of a rainy day.

EXPERIMENT WITH BACKLIGHTING

Things that are translucent, or that let light through, seem to glow when they are lit from behind. Notice the spurt of water and the autumn leaves.

Backlighting carves out very sharp silhouettes and adds a sense of mystery to these two scenes.

The camera that came with this book will produce very good photos if your subjects are well lit — daylight normally provides ideal conditions. But you may not get the best results if you try to use this camera inside or even outside on a very dark, cloudy day.

Now we are getting to the really interesting stuff — the image itself. The organization or arrangement of different elements in a photograph is called *composition*.

When you take a picture of a landscape or of objects that don't move, you have time to plan your photo. But often, there may be one or several elements that move in your viewfinder. You have to be patient in order to release the shutter at the right moment. One second later and the image will be different.

You'll get better results if you limit yourself to one point of interest.

It will take a bit of practice before you get a feel for timing. That is why it's best to begin by taking photographs of scenes without too many elements or too much movement. Most of the time, the best photos are also the simplest! A photograph that is too busy is often very confusing.

Here is an example of confusing composition — there are many elements in this picture, but we are not drawn to any one of them in particular.

These photographs are very simple. We understand right away what the photographer is trying to show us.

If you can, take the time to move around your subject. Change positions; vary the height of your camera; frame the picture vertically by placing the camera on its side; move farther away from your subject or get even closer. By experimenting you will find the way to take the right photograph, the one that will show exactly what you want it to.

When you look through the viewfinder, don't concentrate just on the main subject. Think also about what is in front and behind your subject: the *foreground* and the *background*. If you ignore them, you may end up with unwanted elements in your photograph.

Sometimes it is best to frame the picture vertically.

This photograph is especially nice with the flowers in the foreground.

With a little practice, you will even be able to choose the elements in the foreground and in the background so that they enhance your main subject.

Problems can often be solved simply by moving either the subject or the camera.

This photo is not quite right. Besides being out of focus, the trash does not make a very nice background for the photograph.

Now that's better! It was a matter of asking the children to move a little to the right.

You don't always have to place your main subject right in the center of the photograph. It is often nicer to move your subject within the frame to include another element. A second person, a building, a shadow or a simple splash of color may be enough to add a sense of harmony.

HERE ARE THREE EXAMPLES OF SIMPLE, WELL- BALANCED COMPOSITION.

Pay close attention to the colors, shapes, patterns and textures of the things around you: they will give rhythm and harmony to your photos.

COLOR

It is amazing what you can do with color film! Look at the impact of color on these pictures.

PATTERNS AND TEXTURES

Repeating the same pattern or texture can really enhance your photo.

HERE'S A HELPFUL HINT:
LIMIT YOURSELF TO ONE OR TWO COLORS
FOR A DRAMATIC EFFECT.

Lines

Vertical and diagonal lines can make your photos more dynamic.

Converging lines (lines that lead to the same point) draw our attention, inviting us to come inside the photograph.

To draw attention to your subject, try the *frame-within-the-frame* trick. Fill the foreground with dark foliage or use a window frame or doorway, as shown in these photos.

If you take a picture of something very big (a statue, a building or a cliff, for example), include another element in the frame — something that will give us an idea of the true size.

Now we know how big the statue is!

PHOTOGRAPHING PEOPLE

The world around you is full of interesting subjects. There is no limit to what you can do with your camera. You can take photographs to record your memories, to create something different, or just to have fun. But a photo can also tell a story about your subject, whether it is a person, place or thing.

Just remember the one golden rule of photography: take your camera with you wherever you go and be on the lookout!

PORTRAITS

Budding photographers often start out taking pictures of people. To take good portraits, be sure to get close enough to your subject.

Lost in the field.

But don't get too close. To get a sharp image with a fixed focus camera like yours, you must stand at least 5 feet (1.5 meters) away. Your viewfinder will show you how the picture will be framed.

Off with her head!

Don't take shots of people under strong, direct sunlight. It will create hard shadows on their faces. Ask the person to move into the shade. Also, remember that a cloudy sky will filter the sun's rays and provide more favorable light.

A perfect pose!

22

Make sure there are no strange things in the background that seem attached to your subject. There seems to be a tree growing out of this girl's head!

For a close-up of a person, a vertical shot is often best.

If you want lively, natural portraits of your friends and family, try to catch them in real-life situations, without them knowing that you are snapping their picture!

For posed portraits, encourage the person to relax. Make sure she is in a comfortable position, and chat with her about this and that: she will feel more at ease in front of the camera and you will get better results.

Whatever you do, wait for the right moment and the right expression on your subject's face before you press the shutter.

MAKE SURE YOU TAKE MORE THAN ONE PICTURE OF YOUR SUBJECT; YOU MAY WASTE A BIT OF FILM, BUT YOU'LL INCREASE YOUR CHANCES OF SUCCESS.

For a group photo, limit the number of people in the frame. If there are too many people, you'll have to move so far back that you won't be able to recognize them once the photo is developed.

Make sure that you can see everyone's head. To attract everyone's attention, you can always try the "**Watch the birdie!**" trick, but you might have better luck blowing a whistle that you have just taken out of your pocket.

It's always fun to take pictures of your friends and family. They are usually eager subjects who enjoy the game of photography as much as you do. But if you want to photograph someone you don't know, first ask permission. People don't like their picture being taken without them knowing, but usually they will gladly pose if you ask them nicely.

And why not offer to send them a copy?

This fisherman was taken by surprise, and it shows!

On the other hand, we asked this bus driver for permission to take his photo and look at the wonderful smile we got!

LANDSCAPE PHOTOS

People are often disappointed to find that their vacation pictures do not reflect the wonderful landscapes that they remember. No doubt they took the pictures without taking the time to observe the scene first. The camera can only capture a small part of any landscape.

Take the time to frame your picture to include elements that will say something about the place.

Lighting is very important in landscape photography. If at all possible, come back to the same scene at different times of day and decide when the lighting is best.

The early bird has managed to capture this lovely sunrise.

The sunset lights the sky on fire.

For a really nice picture, lower your camera and include some flowers in the foreground.

Whenever you include the horizon in a photo, keep your camera good and straight, or else it won't appear... horizontal. The same goes for lakes, rivers and seascapes — you don't want to spill water everywhere!

Look at these two photos of the same place, taken at different times of year. What a difference!

IN THE COUNTRY

Let yourself be inspired by the huge spaces and calm of the countryside.

Whatever you do, don't forget your camera on your trip to the farm.

There's more than grass growing in this field!!!

Nature holds many wonderful surprises for the wide-eyed photographer!

IN THE CITY

The city is a great place to take photos.

Lines can be found everywhere and they can really bring your photos to life. Experiment with taking shots from unusual angles.

You can have all kinds of fun with the reflections cast by mirrored buildings and store windows!

You can show the contrast between older and more modern buildings.

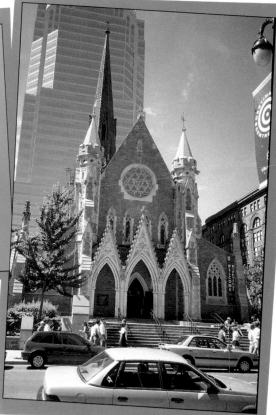

This panorama is enough to make even a bird dizzy. But it was not taken from an airplane, but from the top of the highest skyscraper in town.

The city would be a sad, quiet place without all these people to bring it to life.

Outdoor markets are always very colorful.

Whether you live in the city or the country, look at your own neighborhood as though you were seeing it for the first time. You might make some interesting discoveries!

STILL LIFE

Whenever we think of a still life, we immediately picture a bouquet of flowers or three apples in a bowl. But take a look around you; there are a whole lot of things that are worth closer inspection.

Something may be of special interest because of what it means to you, or simply because of certain colors and shapes.

Things that seem rather ordinary may turn into extraordinary photos!

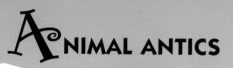

Animals are always a lot more natural in front of the camera than people. But you can't ask them to pose for the photograph! Often you have to be very patient and just a little bit sneaky to take their picture.

If you want a picture of a cat or dog, get down to their level. Either kneel or lie on your stomach for the perfect shot.

Attract your pet's attention by making noises, or ask someone to help you. Sometimes it is best to put yourself out of reach of your pet. Otherwise he might come right up to you when you call him, and you will be too close to take the picture.

Be patient, wait for the right moment, and be quick! He won't repeat the same pose twice!

TAKING PICTURES OF ANIMALS IS A LOT LIKE TAKING PICTURES OF PEOPLE YOU HAVE TO GET CLOSE ENOUGH. SO RESIST THE TEMPTATION TO PHOTOGRAPH BIRDS HIGH UP IN THE SKY. THEY'LL END UP AS LITTLE BLACK DOTS ON A BIG BLUE BACKGROUND.

Don't forget your camera if you're going to the farm...

...or to the zoo!

Taking pictures is a great way to record your happy memories!

Don't miss family gatherings and birthdays!

Try taking holiday pictures from different viewpoints.

You can practically hear the music at this concert.

You'll never forget this day at the fair.

A picture is worth a thousand words!

Hmmm, Dad and Uncle Tom seem very proud of their catch!

At the movie theater or on television, images move quickly, like in real life. But a photograph can also show movement, even though it is a still image.

This picture is blurred, but it is very effective all the same: when you look at it, you are transported onto this crazy ride, right next to these kids.

These photos make the action seem frozen, as though time had stopped all of a sudden. You can create this effect thanks to your camera's fast, pre-set shutter speed.

In this photo the subject is sharp yet the background is blurred; this gives us the impression of speed. Here is how you can take a *panned* shot like this with your camera.

Follow the moving subject in your viewfinder. About half-way through his movement, gently release the shutter but keep following him for a couple of seconds.

In this photo, the camera has captured the children playing, but the movement of the leaves has also left its trace on the film, showing us all the action of the scene.

For some really fun photographs, ask your friends to pose in strange positions, to disguise themselves, or to give you their funniest faces.

You don't need a magic wand to make your friend as tiny as a mouse!

If only I had four hands!

Don't throw away your mistakes! You can keep them to make a funny collage!

Here's a brilliant way to make your own personal puzzle: have one of your close-up photos enlarged, then glue it onto a piece of cardboard of the same size. Using a ruler and a sharp knife (ask an adult for help), cut out different shapes. There you have it! Now can you put it back together again?

THE MOST COMMON MISTAKES

Everyone makes mistakes, even professional photographers. But if you read the next section carefully, you won't miss that once-in-a-lifetime photo of your sister...and you'll save yourself lots of film!

Before you take your first shot, make sure the lens cap is open all the way.

After you have properly loaded your film, make sure to wind it to frame number 1 before you take a picture. Otherwise you may expose only half of your negative, and end up with something like this:

Make sure that there is nothing directly in front of the lens when you take a picture. Look out for fingers, long hair and camera straps especially — you may not see them in the viewfinder, but they might hide a part of your image.

Stand at a good distance from your subject:

not too far...

...not too close.

Remember, you must be at least 5 feet (1.5 meters) away.

Make sure there is enough
light on your subject.

When the sun is lower in the
sky, the shadows are longer.
Be careful not to include your
shadow in the photograph!

Above all, don't open the back of your
camera before the film is rewound com-
pletely into its cassette: the light could
ruin your photos.

Last but not least

Don't let your beautiful pictures collect dust at the bottom of your drawer! Why not have your favorite photos enlarged and then frame them yourself? You can find frames that are already cut to the right dimensions, with or without glass. Or, you can gently glue your photo to a piece of cardboard.

The rest of your interesting photos can go into an album. That way they will be protected, and you can show your friends your entire collection.

What a great gift! Have duplicates made of your best portraits and offer them to your subjects!

As long as you have your negatives, you can always have copies of your photos made. So identify them and keep them in a dry place, where they won't collect any dust. A shoe box will do the trick just fine. You should keep your negatives in the envelopes they came in, and label them with the date and the subject (December 1996 — Christmas at Grandma's). That way they will be easier to find when you want to enter your first photo contest!

44

THERE! NOW YOU KNOW ALL MY SECRETS, AND IT'S TIME FOR YOU TO FLY SOLO. THE WORLD IS YOURS TO CAPTURE IN PICTURES. JUST OPEN YOUR EYES AND CLICK AWAY!

GOODBYE

AND

GOOD LIGHT!

Background: The part of a photograph that is behind the main subject.

Backlighting: Throwing light on a subject from behind.

Composition: The arrangement or organization of all the elements in a photograph.

Developing: The chemical treatment of an image that makes it appear on film or on photographic paper.

Exposure: Light passing through the lens to reach the film in the camera.

Film: A strip of plastic coated with special materials that react to light to record the image seen by the camera.

Film speed: The time it takes for a particular kind of film to react to light. Film speed is measured by an ISO number.

Fixed focus camera: With this camera, you don't need to adjust the lens to get a sharp image depending on your distance from the subject.

Flash: A small electronic lamp powered by battery. It is used to produce artificial light when there is not enough sunlight available to take a picture.

Foreground: The part of a photograph that is in front of the main subject.

ISO number: ISO stands for International Standards Organization. The ISO number on a roll of film measures the film speed. The smaller the number, the slower the film.

Landscape: A view or photograph of scenery. Also used to describe a horizontal photo, where the width is greater than the height.

Lens: A curved piece of glass or plastic that bends light entering the camera so that an image is recorded onto the film. It is the eye of your camera.

Negatives: An exposed film is first developed into negatives. On the negatives, images appear reversed: light parts appear dark and dark parts appear light, while colors are replaced by their complementary colors. The negative is then projected onto photographic paper, where the colors appear as they did when the photo was taken.

Panning: Moving the camera horizontally to follow a subject in the viewfinder. By releasing the shutter halfway through the subject's movement, the action is recorded on the film.

Panorama: A wide, unbroken view of a surrounding region.

Portrait: A close-up picture of a person or animal. Also used to describe a vertical photograph, where the height is greater than the width.

Printing: Projecting an image onto light-sensitive paper to produce a photograph. Once the paper has been exposed to light, it is taken through a series of chemical processes that will make the image visible to the human eye.

Shutter: A device in a camera that lets light in to expose the film and record the image. It works like a curtain. Depending on how fast it opens and shuts (the shutter speed), more or less light will enter.

Still life: A photograph, painting or drawing of inanimate objects.

Telephoto lens: A camera lens that acts like a telescope, making subjects far away appear much closer than they really are.

Viewfinder: The little window on your camera that allows you to see what will be in the photograph. On your camera, the view differs slightly from what is seen by the lens.

Wide-angle lens: a camera lens that can fit more into the picture, giving you the impression of being farther away from your subject.

INDEX

NOTES